CW00657216

OTHER HELEN EXLEY GIFTBOOKS

Be What You Believe In
Personal Values
The Real Meaning of Success
Words on Courage
Words on a Simple Life

Printed simultaneously in 2002 by Helen Exley Giftbooks
in Great Britain and Helen Exley Giftbooks LLC in the USA.

12 11 10 9 8 7 6 5

ISBN 978-1-86187-305-7

Quotations selected by Helen Exley. Printed in China
Illustrated by Angela Kerr.

**Helen Exley Giftbooks, 16 Chalk Hill, Watford,
Herts WD19 4BG, UK.**
www.helenexleygiftbooks.com

Acknowledgements: The publishers are grateful for permission to reproduce copyright
material. Whilst every reasonable effort has been made to trace copyright holders, we
would be pleased to hear from any not acknowledged. TED LODER: from
"The narrow way of trust" in *Wrestling the Light* by Ted Loder. © 1991 Innisfree
Press. JOHN MASEFIELD: "An Epilogue". Reprinted by permission of The Society
of Authors as the Literary Representative of the Estate of John Masefield. **PAM
BROWN: © Helen Exley, 2002.**

The Value of Integrity

A HELEN EXLEY
GIFTBOOK

In the war
between falsehood
and truth,
falsehood wins
the first battle and
truth the last.

MUJIBUR RAHMAN

If rascals knew
the advantages of virtue,
they would become honest.

BENJAMIN FRANKLIN

*Ninety-nine lies
may help you,
but the hundredth
will give you away.*

HAUSA

Truth conquers all....

LATIN PROVERB

Use no hurtful deceit;
think innocently
and justly and,
if you speak, speak
accordingly.

BENJAMIN FRANKLIN

You should always
keep your word.
All the setbacks in life
come only because
you don't
keep your word....

SIVANANDA

*Truth and love
are two of the most powerful
things in the world;
and when they both
go together
they cannot easily
be withstood....*

RALPH CUDWORTH

*Much sheer effort
goes into avoiding truth:
left to itself,
it sweeps in like the tide.*

FAY WELDON,
FROM
"THE RULES OF LIFE"

*There is
nothing so powerful
as truth....*

DANIEL WEBSTER

If you propose

to speak, always

ask yourself – is it true,

is it necessary,

is it kind?....

GAUTAMA BUDDHA
(5 6 3 - 4 8 3 B.C.)

BEING TRUE
TO YOURSELF

*Whatever games are played
with us, we must play no
games with ourselves, but
deal in our privacy with the
last honesty and truth.*

RALPH WALDO EMERSON
(1803-1882)

This above all: to thine own self be true.

WILLIAM SHAKESPEARE

Everything's a circle. We're each responsible for our own actions. It will come back.

BETTY LAVERDURE

When you betray somebody else, you also betray yourself.

ISAAC BASHEVIS SINGER

*I am not bound to win but
I am bound to be true.
I am not bound to succeed
but I am bound to live up
to what light I have. I must
stand with anybody that
stands right: stand with him
while he is right and
part with him when he
goes wrong.*

ABRAHAM LINCOLN
(1809-1865)

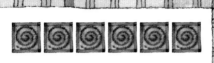

*E*mpower me... to exercise
the authority of honesty,
rather than to defer
to power, or deceive
to get it; to influence
someone for justice,
rather than impress anyone
for gain.

TED LODER

Our fathers gave us many laws, which they had learned from their fathers. These laws were good. They told us to treat all people as they treated us; that we should never be the first to break a bargain; that it was a disgrace to tell a lie; that we should speak only the truth....

CHIEF JOSEPH
(1830-1904)

INSINCERITY

No man, for any considerable period, can wear one face to himself, and another to the multitude, without finally getting bewildered as to which may be the true.

NATHANIEL HAWTHORNE, FROM "THE SCARLET LETTER"

The most exhausting thing in life is being insincere.

ANNE MORROW LINDBERGH
(1906-2001)

...Your health is
bound to be affected
if day after day you say
the opposite of what
you feel, if you grovel
before what you dislike,
and rejoice at what
brings you nothing
but misfortune.

BORIS PASTERNAK

Truth
never falters
or fails;
it is our faith
that fails.

MARY BAKER EDDY

There is
no negotiation
with truth....

FERDINAND LASSALLE

Truth will always triumph; do not doubt this in the least....

SATHYA SAI BABA

*Goodness is the
only investment
that never fails.*

HENRY DAVID THOREAU
(1817-1862)

*Truth, Life, and Love
are formidable,
wherever thought,
felt, spoken,
or written....
They are the victors.*

MARY BAKER EDDY

TRUST

I have seen flowers
come in stony places
And kind things done
by men with ugly faces,
And the gold cup won
by the worst horse
at the races,
So I trust, too.

JOHN MASEFIELD

To be a good human being
is to have a kind of openness
to the world, an ability
to trust uncertain things
beyond your control.

MARTHA NUSSBAUM

ONE PERSON WHOM WE CAN TRUST UTTERLY

A blessed thing
is for any man or woman
to have a friend; one
human soul whom we can
trust utterly; who knows
the best and the worst
of us, and who loves us

*in spite of all our faults;
who will speak the honest
truth to us, while the world
flatters us to our face,
and laughs at us
behind our back.*

CHARLES KINGSLEY
(1819–1875)

It is better
to suffer wrong
than to do it,
and happier
to be sometimes
cheated
than not to trust.

SAMUEL JOHNSON,
FROM "THE RAMBLER"

*It is better
to be deceived
by one's friends
than to deceive
them.*

JOHANN VON GOETHE
(1749-1832)

THE TRUST OF THOSE WE LOVE

How desperately we wish to maintain our trust in those we love! In the face of everything, we try to find reasons to trust. Because losing faith is worse than falling out of love.

SONIA JOHNSON

That quiet mutual gaze of a trusting husband and wife is like the first moment of rest or refuge from a great weariness or a great danger.

GEORGE ELIOT
(MARY ANN EVANS)
(1819-1880)

She is the sort of grandma that if you tell her a secret she will never tell anyone.

JULIA THOMSON, AGE 11

*It does not
require many words
to speak the truth.*

CHIEF JOSEPH
(1830-1904)

*The language
of truth is
unadorned....*

MARCELLINUS
AMMIANUS

*Truth always
expresses itself
with the greatest
simplicity....*

PIERRE SCHMIDT

TRYING TO
KEEP TRUTHFUL

*My soul naturally shuns
a lie, and hates even
the thought of one. I feel
an inward shame and
a sharp remorse if an
untruth happens to escape
me – sometimes it does
if the occasion is
unexpected, and I am
taken unawares.*

MICHEL DE MONTAIGNE
(1 5 3 3 - 1 5 9 2) ,
FROM "ESSAYS"

*Falsehood is so easy;
truth so difficult....*

GEORGE ELIOT
(MARY ANN EVANS)
(1819-1880)

*The voice of
conscience is so delicate
that it is easy to stifle it;
but it is also so clear
that it is impossible
to mistake it.*

MME DE STAÎL

Truth

makes the face

of that person

shine who speaks

and owns it....

ROBERT SOUTH

*Integrity rings
like fine glass. True, clear
and reassuring.*

PAM BROWN, B.1928

Never give up

on anybody.

HUBERT H. HUMPHREY

*B*etter trust all,
and be deceived,
And weep that trust,
and that deceiving;
Than doubt one heart,
that, if believed,
Had blessed one's life
with true believing.

FRANCES ANNE KEMBLE,
FROM "FAITH"

NOT EVERYONE
CAN FACE ALL THE TRUTH
ALL THE TIME

*Keep in mind that 99.44
percent of the truth
is about as big a dose as
anyone can handle.
The other .56 percent is
lethal. Resist the temptation
to disclose the deadly part
of the message.*

NICHOLAS V. IUPPA,
FROM
"MANAGEMENT BY GUILT"

*Truthfulness so often goes
with ruthlessness.*

DODIE SMITH

*It is terrible to destroy a
person's picture of himself
in the interests of truth
or some other abstraction.*

DORIS LESSING

"ONE SHOULD NOT SPEAK WHAT IS TRUE..."

*One should speak
what is true; one should
speak what is sweet;
one should not speak
what is true if it is
not sweet or what is sweet
if it is false;
this is the ancient law....*

MANU

Take the life-lie away from
the average man and
straight away you take
away his happiness.

HENRIK IBSEN,
FROM "THE WILD DUCK"

*There are few
nudities so
objectionable as
the naked truth.*

AGNES REPPLIER,
FROM "COMPROMISES"

CORRUPTION

Do you know that the tendrils of graft and corruption have become mighty interlacing roots so that even men who would like to be honest are tripped and trapped by them.

AGNES SLIGH TURNBULL,
FROM
"THE GOLDEN JOURNEY"

When gain
is put before integrity,
society crumbles.

PAM BROWN, B.1928

Corruption is like a
ball of snow, when once set
a rolling it must increase.

C.C. COLTON (1780-1832)

THE POISON
OF THE HALF-TRUTH

*Falsehood is never so
successful as when
she baits her hook
with truth, and no opinions
so falsely mislead us
as those that are not
wholly wrong....*

C. C. COLTON (1780-1832)

This is the world of the short cut, the evasive answer, the cut corner. Integrity has to hold on tips to survive.

PAM BROWN, B.1928

The thing from which the world suffers just now more than from any other evil is not the assertion of falsehood, but the endless and irresponsible repetition of half-truths.

G.K. CHESTERTON
(1874-1936)

TRUTH DOES NOT CHANGE

When a government loses its integrity the times are dangerous. When the populace accept the loss the times are desperate.

PAM BROWN,
B.1928

*Truth
does not change
because it is,
or is not, believed
by a majority
of the people....*

GIORDANO BRUNO

Reputation, reputation, reputation! O, I have lost my reputation! I have lost the immortal part of myself, and what remains is bestial.

WILLIAM SHAKESPEARE
(1564-1616),
FROM "OTHELLO"

A reputation for good
judgement, for fair dealing,
for truth, and for rectitude,
is itself a fortune.

HENRY WARD BEECHER
(1813-1887), FROM
"PROVERBS FROM PLYMOUTH
PULPIT", 1887

Integrity is not honoured
in a society where the
greatest virtue is never
being found out.

PAM BROWN, B.1928

... FROM THE HEART

Spiritual empowerment is
evidenced in our lives by our
willingness to tell ourselves
the truth, to listen to the truth
when it's told to us, and to
dispense truth as lovingly
as possible, when we feel
compelled to talk from
the heart.

CHRISTINA BALDWIN,
FROM
"LIFE'S COMPANION..."
(1990)

... to teach him to try his best
to avoid the truth – even to press it
when necessary toward the outer
edge of the rainbow – for a reason
of kindness, or of mercy, is far
closer to the heart of truth than
to repeat something accurately
and mercilessly that will cruelly
hurt the feelings of someone.

EMILY POST (1873-1960),
FROM
"CHILDREN ARE PEOPLE"

*I am not afraid
of the pen,
or the scaffold,
or the sword.
I will tell the truth
wherever I please.*

MOTHER JONES

It is hard to hold to integrity
in times of terror –
yet some brave hearts
have endured.

PAM BROWN, B.1928

If, for any reason whatsoever, moral standards are conspicuously and unprecedentedly breached in one area of society, such as the political, it will follow as the night the day that those standards will start collapsing all down the line – in sports, entertainment, education, the armed forces, business and government.

MARGARET HALSEY

*Civilization itself
is founded on integrity
of mind and heart
and action.*

PAM BROWN, B.1928

HYPOCRISY!

*Hypocrisy,
the only evil that walks
invisible.*

JOHN MILTON
(1608-1674)

Better to live as
a rogue and a bum,
a lover all treat
as a joke
to hang out with
a crowd of
comfortable drunks,
than crouch in
a hypocrite's cloak.

MAHSATI
(12TH CENTURY)

THE GREAT LIE
OF SILENCE

*The cruelest lies are often
told in silence.*

ROBERT LOUIS STEVENSON
(1850-1894)

*A lie can travel halfway
around the world
while the truth is
putting on its shoes.*

MARK TWAIN
(1835-1910)

*Truth is not only violated
by falsehood; it may
be outraged by silence.*

HENRI FRÉDÉRIC AMIEL

*Doubts
are more cruel than
the worst of truths.*

MOLIÉRE,
FROM "LE MISANTHROPE"

What loneliness

is more lonely

than distrust?

GEORGE ELIOT
(MARY ANN EVANS)
(1819-1880),
FROM "MIDDLEMARCH"

LIES, LIES, CRUEL LIES

*The telling
of a falsehood
is like a cut of a sabre;
for though
the wound may heal,
the scar of it
will remain....*

SAADI

*Falsehood is
a refuge,
an asylum for
the cruel, the violent,
for consummate
animals.*

ABRAHAM J. HESCHEL

Truth is the only safe ground to stand upon.

ELIZABETH CADY STANTON,
FROM
"THE WOMAN'S BIBLE"

*Truth is incontrovertible.
Panic may resent it;
ignorance may deride it;
malice may distort it;
but there it is....*

WINSTON CHURCHILL
(1874-1965)

Truth burns up error.

SOJOURNER
TRUTH

The only real

satisfaction there is,

is to be growing up

inwardly all the time,

becoming more just,

true, generous, simple,

manly, womanly,

kind, active.

JAMES FREEMAN CLARKE
(1810-1888)

I WOULD BE TRUE

I would be true,
for there are those
that love me
I would be true,
for there are those
that care....

HOWARD ARNOLD WALTER

I have a good heart,
and I want no mistake
made this time,
to live with a
good heart
and talk truth.

CAPTAIN JACK

JUST BE
WHAT YOU ARE

*Just be what you are
and speak from your
guts and heart – it's
all a person has.*

HUBERT H. HUMPHREY

Don't
compromise
yourself.
You are all
you've got.

JANIS JOPLIN
(1943-1970)

Truth is like sugar cane:
even if you chew it for
a long time, it is still sweet.

MALAGASY PROVERB

The ideals which
have lighted my way,
and time after time have
given me new courage
to face life cheerfully,
have been kindness,
beauty, and truth....

ALBERT EINSTEIN
(1879-1955)

"Beauty is truth,
truth beauty – that is all
ye know on earth,
and all ye need to know."

JOHN KEATS (1795-1820)